# WHEN GOD WAS MAN

# WHEN
# GOD
## WAS
# MAN

## *J. B. PHILLIPS*

## ABINGDON PRESS
*New York*   ·   *Nashville*

WHEN GOD WAS MAN

*Library of Congress Catalog Card Number: 54-11680*

B

SET UP, PRINTED, AND BOUND BY THE
PARTHENON PRESS, AT NASHVILLE,
TENNESSEE, UNITED STATES OF AMERICA

# CONTENTS

# I

# OUR IDEA OF CHRIST

THE SCOPE OF THESE SEVEN SHORT CHAP-
ters is to consider the ministry of Christ, that
is, the actual work done by that Man who is
so alive in the pages written nearly two thousand years ago.

In this first chapter I want to make some
preliminary remarks. First, it is very important that you and I should have the right
mental picture of that character and personality. Probably we are all on our guard against
the stylized picture that you get in many
stained-glass windows and religious pictures.
Let us hope we are also on our guard against
the rather soft and sentimental picture of the
same Person presented to us in some of our
hymns.

But what is quite likely to slip past our guard is our own mental picture. We may not realize how far removed it can be from the character actually portrayed by Matthew, Mark, Luke, and John. Now the best of us have only a rather imperfect grasp of what Christ was and is like, but we can at least check what we believe and imagine by referring to the actual records which, in the providence of God, have been handed down to us.

If it is true, as the scripture says, that "Jesus Christ is the same yesterday, today and forever," then we have no right to modify or alter those early portraits. We simply must not read back into those stories what we think ought to have been there. On the other hand there is no reason at all why, after studying those records closely, we should not allow our God-given faculties of imagination to deepen our understanding.

Many people claim to have a sense of Christ's presence. When they pray, he is with them; as they meet life and all its strains and difficulties, he is their companion and guide.

This sense of the living Christ being with people is so widespread that it is to my mind one of the finest evidences of the truth of the Christian faith. The Man whose earthly life we are going to study is alive today.

Yet even here we need to be quite sure that the figure held in our imaginations is really of the same quality, with the same characteristics, as the Jesus Christ of the Gospels. For it is by no means unusual to find people holding a conception of Christ which is only partially true to the actual revelation of himself. Such an imaginative portrait built up in the mind may easily be nothing more than a superconscience. It may be narrow and puritanical where Christ in fact was not. It may have convenient blind spots toward our own failures, which Christ never had or has. It may be soft where Christ was hard, and, strange as it may sound, it may be stern where Christ was most gentle.

I would very earnestly ask you to check your conception of Christ, the image of him which as a Christian you hold in your mind, with the actual revealed Person who can be seen and studied in action in the pages of the Gospels. It may be of some value to hold in our minds a bundle of assorted ideals to influence and control our conduct. But surely we need to be very careful before we give that "bundle" the name of Jesus Christ the Son of God.

Next let us be sure of what it is we are looking at when we study that unique character. Jesus himself once said to Philip, "He that hath seen me hath seen the Father." This means that Jesus was revealing, in this present time-and-space setup, the nature and the character of God—in so far as he can be revealed in a human being. When we study the life of Christ, we are in fact seeing God focused in a human life. So that the way he acts, the things he teaches, the things he loves and the things he hates, indeed every mortal thing that he does or says, are of the very highest importance to us if we are to know what God is like.

I may be wrong, but it therefore seems to me that the actual physical and geographical background is not of the highest importance. The setting is in a sense "accidental." It happened to be Palestine two thousand years ago, but it might just as well have been India, or South Africa, or Germany, or China, as far as the real significance is concerned. It won't therefore help us very far to understand the meaning of that life if we study Palestinian customs all those years ago. It will help us far more if we study how that Man met human situations which are a permanent part of the life of mankind in all ages and in all places. We are watching something quite unique. For the first time in the history of our planet God himself (reduced, as it were, in stature to one of his own creation) can be seen doing and saying in a particular context things which represent his eternal and changeless character.

If we dare to study this life with open minds, we may easily get some surprises. We may find that our notions of being good by no means always correspond with his ideas. The way we set about living, the things we most highly value, the actions we most highly praise, all these and many other things are by no means always endorsed by the teaching of Jesus Christ. Indeed to our amazement we may

11

story with which perhaps you are only too familiar. You don't need to know any Greek or to be very clever to do this, though you may be surprised to find that it is quite hard work. But it is most rewarding and revealing, for you will find that you have no longer a faraway Figure existing, as it were, in a most holy legend. You will find, as any translator finds, that this disturbing, challenging, and yet attractive Figure comes to life all over again.

I hope then that you will understand what it is I am suggesting in this introduction. It is simply that even those who have been Christians for years quite frequently hold in their minds an idea and a conception of Jesus Christ which do not square with those recorded in the Gospels. I am not blaming them for this. I am simply saying that I know it to be a fact in my experience.

That is why it is necessary for us not once, but again and again, to go back to the inspired words of the Gospels and see what he really was like. If that means throwing overboard some of the ideas we have previously held or

13

# II

# HEALTH FOR A DISEASED WORLD

THIS CHAPTER IS THE FIRST OF SIX glimpses which we are going to take at what is commonly called the ministry of Jesus Christ. I am not so sure, by the way, that I am very keen on that word "ministry"; it has a certain technical, or even professional, flavor. I should much prefer it if we could simply say that we are going to look at six different aspects of what Christ did and said, at what actually happened when God, focused in human form, emerged from the village in which he had worked and came into daily contact with the people living at that time.

If we start with Mark's Gospel, which was

the first one to be written, we cannot help noticing that the early work of Christ is almost entirely a matter of healing the body. There was very little knowledge of medicine in those days, and we can safely guess that disease of all kinds was very common.

We are looking at love incarnate, at one whose heart was undoubtedly filled with pity and the desire to help. Or, to put it slightly differently, we are also looking at complete wholeness and health coming into contact with what Mark calls "all manner of sickness and disease among the people." Enormous crowds gathered wherever Christ went, and, we read, "he healed them all."

Now to our nice tidy minds the Gospel stories are maddeningly unchronological. You have only to read one of the other Gospels, particularly John, just after you have read Mark, to see what I mean. Consequently we cannot be sure whether this healing work occurred *before* the teaching about the Kingdom or whether it went on at intervals all the time. It seems to me highly probable that the Source of all health and wholeness would prove a radiant center of healing in a little world where disease was so prevalent. There are plenty of incidents to suggest that, whenever people approached him in honest faith, their physical diseases were healed.

This power of physical healing, which the Gospels assure us Christ imparted at any rate for a time to his disciples, is very much in the minds of many people today. Compared with that instantaneous insight and equally instantaneous healing, modern medicine, for all its marvels, seems clumsy, laborious, and complicated. This is not the place to do more than indicate the problem. But since when Christ walked the earth the link between his power to heal and the sufferer was a faith in his power to heal, many responsible Christians today are feeling that we have not paid nearly enough attention to the power of a faith in Christ.

After all, all healing takes place because of the natural power of the body to heal itself. In the actual presence of Christ this power was evidently so stimulated that the body was often able to throw off instantaneously the disease or disability. Modern medicine and

17

surgery can do no more than remove the causes which are preventing the body reverting to health. It could easily be that this natural force of recovery could be enormously enhanced if there were real faith in the active, operative power of Christ.

Now we notice that this contact of whole-ness with disease and sickness of every kind was not limited to the physical. Christ did not only heal disease. He also "cast out devils." Modern people are quick to ridicule the idea current in Christ's day that all forms of men-tal disease were due to "possession by devils." But if you have had contact with those who are what we call insane, or even with someone who, as we still say, is "beside himself" with furious temper, you certainly get the strong impression that there is some other spiritual force making that person speak and behave in a way quite alien to his normal real self.

Now Jesus plainly accepted the terminology of his day. Even if he had known it, there would not have been the slightest use for him to quote modern psychological jargon, which, may I remind you, may one day be as outdated as the old-fashioned term "devil-possessed." With unerring instinct he addressed himself to that storm center of the personality, that monstrous, and even violent, second self (which for various reasons had become established within the personality), and commanded it to "come out." The result was an instantaneous cure.

This may well make us marvel when we compare it with modern psychiatric methods, which may take months or even years. A friend of mine, who is in the first rank of psychiatrists, once told me that if a patient could see and accept the love of God, his recovery would be enormously accelerated or even be instantaneous. But unhappily those who are psychologically ill are often under a kind of dark cloud which prevents this from happening. Yet this is plainly what did happen in the actual presence of the love of God focused in a human being. Christ was able to go straight in and command the disruptive, violent, and dangerous elements to dissolve.

At the moment all that modern psychiatry can do is to help the patient sort out and deal with those discordant elements in his own personality which are causing him such mental agony. But I for one do not believe he is ever really healed until he has found for himself what he really is, a beloved son of God.

But the work of Christ, as we all know, was not confined to healing men's bodies or relieving the tortures of their minds. He came to make them spiritually whole, to change them from little self-centered individuals into men who knew that they were sons of God, and to show them how they could live up to such a high calling. At rare moments when we draw near to God, we ourselves become aware of our own deeply entrenched self-love. We realize not only the obvious sins but our secret pride, our mean hypocrisies, and our frightening unwillingness to do anything about them.

Now to Christ all this must have been painfully obvious all the time, and, one cannot help feeling, must have oppressed him very considerably. Yet it would also appear that he could discern the light of the real man shining beneath the shadows of sin and self-love, for in fact we very rarely find him calling men sinners. It is almost as though he calls to that little hidden but real self to come out from behind the defenses, pretenses, and evasions and to stand up and follow him. Doubtless those who did so felt, sooner or later, a strong sense of their own sinfulness; but it is quite remarkable that Christ does not call them sinners. Yet if you think about it, there was no need. In the presence of perfect health the sick and under-nourished, the deformed and the diseased, do not need to have their condition underlined. Except in rare cases Christ did not need to draw attention to a man's sins.

There is, however, a notable exception. In the case of the religious leaders, the entrenched self-righteous, we find this perfect wholeness lashing out with a tongue of biting scorn. It is as though some violent means was needed to pierce the matted layers of years of hypocrisy and false religion, and stab awake the real man within. For such men wholeness could not begin until their armor of complacency had been stripped away.

Picture then in this first glimpse of God at work in human surroundings perfect wholeness of body, mind, and spirit moving in a world distressed, warped, and blind. His love and pity are unfailing; his insight is utterly penetrating; his truth is pure and uncompromising.

It is clear from the Gospel records that many accepted healing of body and mind, but far fewer were willing to let him touch the central citadel, the much-beloved self. Yet we cannot believe that his design was anything less than making men whole, healed in body and mind and restored in soul to become sons of God.

# III

# THE AUTHORITY OF TRUTH

IN THIS SECOND GLIMPSE OF JESUS CHRIST'S work I suggest we look at it from another angle. In the last chapter we considered him as perfect wholeness coming into a world ridden with disease and deformity of body, mind, and soul. Now I want to consider him as incarnate truth coming into this world. It is not all darkness; God has already spoken through the consciences, the intuitions, and the imaginations of men. But naturally, compared with his perfect light, the scene *is* dark. There is muddled thinking; there are wrong ideas about life and God, quite apart from man's definitely evil ways of thinking which the Light is bound to reveal for what they are.

If we did not know the answer already to

some extent, how thrilled and excited we should be! Now that God comes in person, what shall we find? Have men's best ideas all been misguided? Is there a plane of truth higher than the best to which we can reach? Even though we know a little of what he said, I feel I must underline what it is we are see-ing—the Truth coming into the world of human ideas.

I would suggest to you that there are three lines through which his truth pierces our common ways of thought. I cannot guarantee that this is the order in which he gave them. Indeed I think it probable that he used all three lines of thought throughout his ministry.

The first characteristic of his truth is a kind of clarified common sense. "Of course," we cry, "we knew this all the time!" Yes, we knew it; but it was obscured by the competitive and God-forgetting spirit of the world in which we live.

"Judge not, and you will not be judged." "With what measure ye mete, it shall be measured to you again." "By their fruits ye shall know them." What are these but glimpses of the psychologically obvious? Yet we need to be reminded of them. "If you want to produce good fruit," Christ said in effect, "you must make the tree good." How obvious! Yet how many people attempt to attach good fruits to a tree that is rotten at heart.

Still in this category of common sense I would put his advice to those who wanted the admiration of their fellows. "It is foolish to sit down straightaway in the most honorable seat at a dinner party; there is always a chance that you will have to give up your place to somebody more distinguished than yourself. Why not try the opposite method? Sit down in an undistinguished seat, and then you will have the pleasure of being asked to move up. That is the way to get admiration if you want admiration."

There are plenty of other instances, all sheer down-to-earth common sense, in Christ's teaching. This is tremendously heartening, for it means that the good sense which God has implanted in us is part of the eternal truth of God.

The second and far more disquieting aspect

of truth which he taught was not common sense at all, or at least it may be common sense in the world to which we are going, but here it appears either nonsense or a kind of super-sense.

Consider for a moment what we commonly call the Beatitudes. The word translated "blessed" means almost exactly what we mean by the word "happy," and since most people in this world desire above everything else to be happy, Jesus reveals the attitude of mind and the kind of conduct which lead to real and lasting happiness. Perhaps I can make this contrast sharper if I give you first the beatitudes of many ordinary people. They would run something like this:

Happy are the "pushers": for they get on in the world.

Happy are the hard-boiled: for they never let life hurt them.

Happy are they who complain: for they get their own way in the end.

Happy are the blasé: for they never worry over their sins.

Happy are the slave drivers: for they get results.

Happy are the knowledgeable men of the world: for they know their way around.

Happy are the troublemakers: for they make people take notice of them.

Now in modern language this is what Jesus said:

Happy are the humble-minded, for they already belong to the kingdom of heaven!

Happy are those who know what sorrow means, for they will be given courage and comfort!

Happy are those who claim nothing, for the whole earth will belong to them!

Happy are those who are hungry and thirsty for goodness, for they will be fully satisfied!

Happy are the kindhearted, for they will have kindness shown to them!

Happy are the pure in heart, for they will see God!

Happy are those who make peace, for they will be known as sons of God!

You can hardly have a sharper or more devastating contrast than that. It is almost as

though Jesus is giving here a recipe for happy
and constructive living. The world has tried,
goodness knows, the first lot of beatitudes for
long enough—with the results that we can see
all around us. Many people felt in his day,
just as we may well feel in our day, that it
might be well worth following his revolutionary design for living.

We may fairly imply from the teaching of
the Gospels that here, crystallized in these
Beatitudes, we have the new attitude of mind
and heart which is essential for all those who
want to join Christ in building the kingdom
of God, a kingdom existing in the hearts of
men and women, and which knows no bar-
riers of class, nation, or color. But it is quite
revolutionary, and that is why, as Christ said
many times, we need to start again as little
children, we need to be converted, we need to
change our whole outlook, which is what re-
pentance really means. Highly religious people
like Nicodemus were told that they needed to
be "born again," so fundamental is the change
of outlook that he requires.

All through the teaching of Christ there is

an emphasis on the heart, on the inward attitude, rather than on outward performance.
There was more hope for the tax collector who
realized his own failure than for the righteous
Pharisee who treated God to a recital of his
own virtues.

Now all this is at first sight most disturbing.
We should like Jesus, who was truth in human
form, simply to endorse our best feelings and
give us a little more truth to help us on our
way. He does in fact endorse all that is good
and true in our thinking and our aspiration,
but he tells us that a new quality of living is
necessary if we are not merely to live as sons
of God, but to spread this kingdom of inner
loyalty. His emphasis *is not on being good, but
on following his way*. The goodness is purely a
by-product. This may well shake us—as it was
probably meant to do. But you will search the
Gospels in vain for any exhortation simply to
be good, or be pure, or be honest, or be un-
selfish. Instead Christ says simply again and
again, "Follow me," which means learning a
new technique of living altogether.

But there is another and further aspect of

his teaching which is just as disturbing and which we shall have to consider in the next chapter. It is that a man's relationship with God and his relationship with his fellows are very closely connected. Jesus would not allow true religion to be a luxury or a fantasy or an exercise in a vacuum; it had to be expressed in ordinary life. He was most devastatingly practical.

# IV

# A Down-to-Earth
# Message

WE HAVE BEEN CONSIDERING HOW UN-compromisingly practical Jesus was in his teaching. There is something in all of us which would like religion to be a little "extra," a sort of flower or decoration on the common ground of life. But while it is true that Jesus, like all other religious leaders, taught men to pray, that is, taught them to look away from the world of ordinary sense impressions and to open the heart and spirit to God, yet he is always insistent that religion must be related to life. It is only by contact with God that a better quality of living can be achieved—and Jesus himself, as the records show, spent many hours in communion with God—yet that new quality of life has to be both demonstrated and tested in the ordinary rough and tumble of plain living. It is in ordinary human relationships that the validity of a man's communion with God is to be proved.

Two instances of this down-to-earth quality of Jesus come to mind. The first is that of the young man born with a silver spoon in his mouth who had always had plenty of money, good food, and clothes, and had in fact led a sheltered life. He had kept all the commandments, he was what we would call a good-living young man, and the Gospel tells us that the heart of Jesus warmed toward him.

But some inner voice was warning this young man that all was not well, there was something missing. "What lack I yet?" he cried. I wonder what answer he expected— probably a religious one. Would there be extra religious duties, extra charitable giving, extra pieties of some kind? No, Jesus saw that what he must do was to plunge into life without the cushioning and protection of riches. His goodness, his piety, must be tested with reality. The reply of Jesus is as startling as a sudden explosion. "Sell everything you've got and give the money away, and then come and follow me!" Jesus saw that whatever protects and insulates from firsthand living has to be stripped away before real life can begin.

Much the same thing happened to the lawyer who asked him what he must do to inherit eternal life. This man knew the pith and essence of the commandments. He knew that he must love God with the whole of his personality, and he must love his neighbor with the same love that he naturally had for himself.

But again there is a niggling doubt in his mind that this is not enough. He probably is already nice and kind and hospitable to his neighbors, but he wants to make quite sure how far his obligations really extend. "Who *is* my neighbor?" he asks. Then Jesus tells him that unforgettable story which we know as the parable of the good Samaritan. The sting, the sting of truth, lay in the tail. Instead of telling the man exactly who his neighbor was, Jesus asks him who acted like a neighbor to the man who had been set on by thugs. The an-

one who is both God and man in one person.

Consider for a moment that terrifying parable about forgiveness. I suspect you remember it well. The man who owed his master a debt which he could never repay was generously let off the whole amount. Yet the same servant went out and seized one of his fellow servants who owed him a few paltry shillings and without showing him the least mercy or consideration had him put in prison for debt. His master was furious and punished him with the utmost severity. Jesus concludes with this stern warning: "So likewise shall my heavenly Father do also unto you, if ye from your hearts forgive not every one his brother their trespasses."

And in another place he says, "For if ye from your hearts forgive not your brother his trespasses, neither will my heavenly Father forgive you your trespasses."

This is alarming truth indeed, and the kind of truth that I for one believe is often hushed up; for it is far too penetrating for our liking. Yet in the very Lord's Prayer itself we have all of us said thousands of times, "Forgive us our trespasses *as we forgive* them that trespass against us." I am convinced that Jesus meant us to understand that our relationship with God *can never* be divorced from our relationship with one another.

To my mind this principle is of the very highest importance, and it should be underlined far more than it ever is. It is all too easy for most of us to make a kind of split in our minds whereby one side of us says prayers or sings hymns or worships God in church, or at home, for that matter, while the other side of us remains cold and critical and unloving toward the people whom we meet day by day.

Now though we may not like it, it is just this sort of split which Jesus will not have at any price. It would hardly be an exaggeration to say that it was his insistence on the connection between religion and life which led to his death. His bitterest enemies and the men who eventually got him put to death were those who could not bear his exposure. They were religious to the highest possible degree, but Jesus does not hesitate to call them hypocrites, frauds, play actors, white sepulchers, even children of the devil, because their professed love of God did not issue in love of their fellows.

What I have called Jesus' devastating practicality runs all through his teaching. In the picture that he gives of the Last Judgment you will notice that people are judged not by religion but by their actions or lack of them. Many are surprised to find themselves on the side of the angels. All they have done is to give themselves in love and charity to their fellow men.

But Jesus assures them, "Inasmuch as ye did it unto one of the least of these, ye *did it unto me*." He and humanity are inseparable; the man who says he loves God and hates his brother is now shown to be a liar. For the religious ones who cannot understand how they could ever have seen Christ in any kind of need and failed to minister to him are told, "Inasmuch as ye did it not unto the least of these, ye did it not unto me." They had utterly failed to see that Christ had identified himself with the human race, not with its perfect specimens but *with humanity*—with the blind, the deaf, the dumb, the mentally deficient, the repulsively sick, the refugee, the beggar, and the outcast.

There is truth here to make us furiously think. Suppose Christianity is not a *religion* at all but a way of life, a falling in love with God, and through him a falling in love with our fellows. Of course such a way is hard and costly, but it is also joyous and rewarding even in the here and now. People who follow that way know beyond all possible argument that they are in harmony with the purpose of God, that Christ is with them and in them as they set about his work in our disordered world.

If anyone thinks this is perilous and revolutionary teaching, so much the better. That is exactly what they thought of the teaching of Jesus Christ. The light he brought to bear upon human affairs is almost unbearably brilliant, but it is the light of truth, and in that light human problems can be solved.

# V

# CHRIST'S FATHER AND OURS

AS WE CONSIDER CHRIST'S TEACHING ABOUT the nature of God, we need to remember all the time who it is who is speaking. It is the one who came down from heaven to live actually, though temporarily, in this human scene, and to reveal not only things that we might have guessed or known in our better moments, but certain basic truths about which he never argued.

The first and most important of these things, which is the background of all our living, is that God is our Father. This does not mean of course that he is like a magnified image of our own earthly fathers—indeed people may have had difficult or even unpleasant fathers then as now—but that the *relationship* between God and man can best be grasped by the human mind by thinking of God as an infinitely patient, wise, and loving Father.

I think perhaps it is easier for those who have had or have good parents to accept this, and possibly easier still for those who are lucky enough to be parents themselves. For example, I can remember, when my daughter was very small indeed, appreciating quite poignantly how the infinite love and wisdom of God must regard us faulty, stumbling, and sometimes rebellious human beings.

Of course some superior people claim to be able to imagine God as the infinite Spirit, as infinite light or power. I don't know whether they really manage this, but I do think for most of us ordinary people we have to have some mental conception around which we can group everything we know and learn about God. Certainly we should beware of having too small a God; it is pathetic to see grown-up people still trying to love and worship the idea of God they held when they were young children.

But despite all that experience of life and

the discoveries of science teach us, it still does not seem to me anything but useful to regard God as our heavenly Father. He is doubtless more intellectually our superior than the proud father is of his small son whom he watches crawling on the hearth rug. But on Christ's authority we can say that the *relationship* is the same.

Now this is one of those things that we should not dare to believe if we had not been told of its truth on the authority of the Son of God himself. Have you ever thought what enormous comfort there is in those words of Christ when he said, "If your son were hungry and asked you for bread, you wouldn't give him a stone, or if he asked you for an egg you wouldn't give him a serpent. If you, for all your evil, know how to give good gifts to your children, *how much more* will your heavenly Father give good things to those who ask him?"

You see the incredible comfort of that phrase "how much more." God cannot possibly be less patient, less kind, less painstaking, less tolerant, than we are; he must be infi-

41

nitely more so. And yet, believe me, there are quite a number of Christians who are trying to worship and serve a god whose character is less worthy of honor and respect than the best men and women that we know.

To Jesus Christ the whole of life was to be lived under the eyes and in the care of this infinite love of the heavenly Father. Not a sparrow falls to the ground without his knowing about it, he assured his disciples; and not a hair could fall from their heads without God's knowledge.

This did not mean to Jesus that life was specially protected for those who believe in their heavenly Father. Indeed it plainly was not. Not only did he warn his disciples again and again that following his costly way of life might mean misunderstanding, persecution, or even death; but he himself, whose life had always been one of perfect faith in his heavenly Father, was in no way specially protected when his enemies closed in upon him.

No, what appeared to puzzle Jesus was that so few people were prepared to believe in this constant loving heavenly care. "Their lack of

faith astonished him," we read on one occa-
sion; and at other times he says, "Oh, what a
faithless people you are! How long must I
be with you before you believe?" He even
coined the word "little-faiths"—in gentle
mockery, no doubt—to describe the attitude
of those who followed him.

If we try sincerely and reverently to follow
Christ's mind, it would seem that this blindness on the Godward side both amazed and
distressed him. Where life was lived without
this sense of the fatherhood of God, man's
values became mixed and jumbled and even
downright wrong. Do you remember how he
once cried out, almost in exasperation, I believe, "How *can* you believe so long as you are
receiving honors from one another and not
bothering about the honor that comes from
God alone?"

It is a kind of vicious circle. The less men see
of God their Father, the more they are
swamped by the values of this passing world;
and the more they are swamped, the less chance
there seems to be of their either seeing God
or hearing his Word to them. "There are things

which men think perfectly splendid which are thoroughly detestable in the eyes of God," Christ once reminded men, which is an example of what happens when God the Father is forgotten and the competitive values of the world hold sway.

The cares of this world and the deceitfulness of riches, just as much as actual sins, are capable of choking the spiritual life out of a man. "You cannot have it both ways," Christ says in effect. "No man can serve two masters. You cannot believe in the power of God and the power of money at the same time."

This teaching, then, of God as the Father is predominant in the recorded teaching of Jesus Christ. It is we who give God other titles—"high and mighty, King of kings, Lord of lords," and so on. These are fine-sounding words, but I would suggest to you that perhaps they obscure the real nature of God and his true relationship with us men. We have no right to suppose that the glory of the Father is some supercolossal magnification of earthly glory. Judging from the method of the Incarnation, I should judge that it is of a different quality altogether.

Jesus himself drew a very sharp distinction between this world's scale of honor, power, authority, and so on, and the true, lasting relationships of the Kingdom. After he has mentioned how ordinary earthly rulers are honored and privileged, he says emphatically, *"It shall not be so among you! All ye are brethren. The man who wants to be greatest among you must become the least important; he must become the servant of you all, just as the Son of Man did not come to be ministered unto, but to minister, and to give his life a ransom for many."*

Now this is revolutionary teaching, and as I look back down the long centuries, I find it hard to believe that it has been widely followed. The honors, distinctions, and deferences found in the Church of God bear far too strong a resemblance to the surrounding world for my liking, and probably for yours too.

This teaching of God as the Father runs through a great many of the parables and is fundamental to the Christian way of life. To regard other men as my brothers remains a mere dream, particularly if I do not like them, unless I realize with a kind of salutary humility that *we all have the same Father*.

As this truth dawns upon us, we see that although men are very different in their gifts and abilities, as Jesus himself taught, yet their status before God is the same. After all, compared with his infinite wisdom, the wisest and best of us are only what Christ called "unprofitable servants."

But we are to think of God *as our Father*. There is a confidence in God expressed not only in Christ's life but right through the New Testament which it seems to me we have largely lost today.

I wonder why.

# VI

# STERN WARNINGS—
## AND
# SPLENDID PROMISES

LIKE EVERY GOOD TEACHER, JESUS CHRIST
started from what men knew and led them on
to learn things that they did not know.
Nearly all his parables follow this method of
teaching. But though we read that he con-
tended with the Pharisees and other religious
leaders, it is worth noting that he never argued
about the basic facts of life—about the existence of God or about the existence of human
suffering and sin. He does not waste time in
arguing about them, but he "speaks with authority" because he is the expert speaking on
his own subject. He is the one who came down

from heaven and can speak with complete assurance about spiritual reality.

Now I want to draw your attention to one particular aspect of that reality, that is, his teaching about heaven and hell, eternal life and in fact the general background of eternity against which this little life is set. I have already spoken about Christ's surprise and distress at men's blindness on the Godward side and their almost nonexistent faith in a loving heavenly Father. I think we may fairly guess that he was also surprised and distressed by men's lack of appreciation of what nowadays we should call the "dimension" of eternity. People, then as now, became preoccupied with this world and failed to see the reality of the world to come.

Solid reality to Christ was God and the life of God; the shadowy, the unsubstantial, is this little life set "in time." God was always to Christ "the God of the living" and not of the dead. I don't think, for example, that he was in the least surprised to find himself in conversation with Moses and Elijah on the Mount of Transfiguration.

Now we must not treat this life as a tiresome little interlude to be somehow endured before we enjoy the wonders of the Father's presence. According to the teaching of Christ this life is both important and decisive. It is the spirit in which men live here and now which determines their situation in the next stage of existence.

Sometimes Jesus brought this teaching down to a fine point as in the case of the story of Dives and Lazarus. Notice that he does not hesitate to talk punishment, reward, and compensation in the world that is to come. We get the same note of stern warning about the future when Jesus is talking about "a hand or foot or eye leading us astray." With all his tenderness and sympathy (indeed it is a part of his tenderness and sympathy) he does not hesitate to warn men that there may be parts of their natures which must be firmly and even painfully suppressed if they are to live life as God means them to lead it. It is far better "to get into heaven with one eye than to be thrown into hell-fire with both your eyes intact."

This is a sharp and vivid sentence, as no doubt it is meant to be; and perhaps we might spend a moment considering what "hell-fire" really means. The clue lies, I think, in the word *gehenna,* which in the King James Version is translated "hell fire." In point of fact *gehenna* means the "burning place" and was used to describe the city's rubbish dump outside the wall of Jerusalem. It was the place of waste and decay and destruction. Jesus surely used it symbolically to mean, not a place of torture, but the place for useless rubbish.

The real danger is, not that we might be tortured for endless ages, but that we might be found to be useless and only fit, so to speak, for the celestial rubbish dump. I am talking in picture language here of course, but there is no doubt that Jesus envisaged a real danger that men might find themselves shut out from the joyful purpose of God.

Suppose then that this life is a probationary stage, a training school, a preparation for a far fuller life that is to come. It is surely not unreasonable to think that there may be those who so misuse this stage, and who become so blind and deaf to the call of God's reality, that they make themselves useless for the magnificent high adventure of the next stage of living.

This is of course a very serious and solemn thought, but it seems to me that Christ, with his perfect spiritual insight which was not bounded by the limits of this life, could see the possibility of such a fate. That is why we get such stern warnings against offending little children, for example, or against becoming spiritually proud, complacent, and unloving. It is incarnate Love which gives the warning, for he could see quite plainly the dangers that lie ahead for certain types of living.

That is why I think it is worth our while to look at these warnings which Christ gives, even though they may seem to go against the grain of our modern toleration. We don't want to get back to exaggerated terrors of hell-fire, but we do need to pay attention to the warnings of the Son of God.

Now of course the teaching of Christ about the background of eternity is not merely a series of warnings; very far from it. He speaks quite openly of rewards, of joys, and even of fresh positions and responsibilities in the world that is to come. We can be sure that here he is not guessing, but telling us of what he knows is true. "Give things away now," he says in effect, "your riches, your possessions, your services, even your life itself, and you will be magnificently rewarded in the world that is to come."

For some reason or another we regard the profit motive as somehow indecent. But Jesus is a shrewder psychologist than we are, and he knows that the profit motive is inherent in human nature. What he suggests is not that we should deny its existence but that we should lift it to a much higher level. This is all of a piece with his advice over other fundamentals of human nature—love and fear and ambition, for example. "He knew what was in man," and instead of denying that we have these things in our make-up, he proposed that their basic drive should be used on a new level of living, in following his way.

It would probably pay us to study the sort of things for which Christ promised heavenly reward. Yet it is very important to notice that, although we are at present in the time-and-space setup, in one sense heaven begins in us now. Christ said the kingdom of heaven is "within you," and although it is of course only partially and somewhat blindly established here on earth, yet it really does begin in the here and now.

Listen to these words recorded by John in the fifth chapter and twenty-fourth verse. Jesus said, "He that heareth my word, and believeth on him that sent me, hath everlasting life." Notice the force of the present tense, "*hath* everlasting life." The moment a man's central confidence is shifted from his own efforts to the God who made him, he is linked to the timeless life of God himself, that is, eternal life. To put it bluntly, heaven is not, as we might deduce from some hymns, a "reward for being a good boy." It is continuance and expansion of a quality of life already imparted to the man who believes in Christ and follows his way.

This makes what we call "death" logically of negligible account, *and this is precisely what we find Christ says.* Not only does he claim to be in person the resurrection and the life, but he says that the man who believes in him will *"never see death."* This can mean only that death is not experienced at all by those whose lives are entrusted to him. And that is the sense in which his scandalized hearers understood him at the time.

Now goodness knows people will take certain sayings of Christ absolutely literally when they are trying to prove a point about pacifism or socialism or divorce, but a categorical statement such as that, which will admit of no other meaning, is far too often taken with a grain of salt. But why should it be? Must we always dim the splendor of Christ's promises by our miserable lack of faith? The One who came from heaven, that is, the real world, and was shortly going back to heaven, promises that the same quality of timeless life can be in any man who entrusts his life to the Son of God. Why can't we believe that?

# VII

# Our Reactions to Him

IF WE DID NOT KNOW THE FACTS OF THE case, I think we should probably guess that, if God visited in person this world of his creating, the human response would be tremendous. After all, consider what such a visit gives to men. It brings light into darkness; it brings wholeness and health in place of disorder and disease. It not only means an unforgettable example of living which can be observed and recorded, but it also means the giving of teaching whereby ordinary people can link themselves to the life and purpose of God. It offers boundless possibilities and answers at the deepest possible level our fundamental needs: to love and be loved, to know real and permanent security and to be assured of our proper significance.

Moreover, such a personal visit of God in human form means a reconciliation between God and man; the age-long estrangement between man and God which all religions recognize is finally dissolved. And death, that ancient enemy, that terror of so many minds, is shown to be a conquered foe. "Jesus Christ hath abolished death," as Paul the apostle once wrote triumphantly to his young friend Timothy.

What I have just said is only the briefest résumé of what the personal visit of God could mean to men. The appalling thing is that in fact it has meant so little to so few. The actual event took place nearly two thousand years ago, and even then, in the actual presence of God personified in a human being, we find only a comparative few responding to his call and following his way.

If we could look at this with detachment, we would see that this blindness, this unwillingness to change, this failure to see who Christ was and what he was trying to do, is the measure of the infection, both collective and individual, of human sinfulness. Many today object to the teaching of original sin, but the doctrine really means that we are born into an infected world. How else can you explain the rejection of truth, the unwillingness to believe, and the refusal to follow the new highroad which would lead out of human frustrations and miseries into lives worthy of God the Father?

Surely the old words are true, "This is the condemnation, that light is come into the world, and men loved darkness rather than light, because their deeds were evil." I would suggest that here is a question for our most serious discussion: How is it that, when the Son of God himself entered the world, he was accepted and followed by so small a minority?

As far as we can judge from the Gospel records of Christ's life, there are two main reasons why, as we begin to approach the end of his life, the number of his followers has already dwindled. The first reason for opposition is, I think, the sheer unwillingness to change. The gospel of the Kingdom was and is a revolutionary way of thinking. It calls for a new way of living altogether, with fresh values and a fresh way of looking at life. Even though men may for a moment glimpse the joy and the glory of such living, they also know that it will be costly. They will have to think; they will have to decide; they may have to stand out from the crowd to which they belong; they may have to be unpopular; they will certainly have to be brave.

Alas, the pull of old habit is very strong; and the comfortable humdrum way of living kept and keeps many from doing anything more than vaguely admiring incarnate Truth and Love. The moment the old life is seriously challenged, the moment there is a hint of personal cost or discomfort, men, then as now, relapse, even though rather wistfully, into the old shadows. Social convention and public opinion frequently prove stronger than the call of the Son of God.

And that, by the way, explains why among Christ's followers were found both prostitutes and tax collectors; for these people had already broken with convention and public opinion and had no comfortable cloak of respectability to lose. We would never for one moment have guessed that people like that went into the Kingdom before the good and pious. Yet that is precisely what Christ assured us really happened.

Thus the most effective opposition to the coming of Light into the world was man's frightening preference for the grayness of mediocre living. We might say that "they preferred the half-light because their deeds were a compromise." This deadly apathy, this refusal to commit oneself, to take risks, to suffer pain, to make a stand, to bear responsibility, to give and to serve without counting the cost, this dull gray blanket of noncommittal agnosticism is the biggest enemy of the cause of Christ in our country today.

It is not that men have come to the Light and found the Light faulty or misleading; it is that they have remained in their own comfortable half-light. It is not that they have followed the Way and found its promises empty and its glory and joy mere words. At the most they have admired from a distance and never

WHEN GOD WAS MAN

set foot on the new and exciting, but risky,
way of living. It is never that God has been
proved a failure, but always that men have
preferred the dull, safe little truths of experience to the risky adventure of proving the
shining promises of God.

But there was another and a surprising en-
mity which becomes increasingly evident if we
study the closing scenes of Christ's earthly life.
It came from the leaders of religion. It would
be easy to think of secondary reasons for the
opposition of the scribes and Pharisees and their
friends—they were jealous of Christ's popular-
ity, of his demonstrations of power, of his un-
doubted spiritual authority. But I believe that
the real opposition sprang from a deeper cause
—the opposition between law and love.

Perhaps we can understand the conflict if
we look at it like this. The "good" man, the
man whose god is righteousness, has as his life's
ambition the keeping of rules and commandments and the keeping of himself uncontami-
nated by the world. This sounds admirable,
but as the truth of Christ showed, the whole
of such living, the whole drive and ambition,

the whole edifice, is self-centered. That entire process of effort must be abandoned if a man is to give himself in love to God and his fellows. He must lose his life if he is ever going to find it.

Now to the good-living, the law-abiding, the commandment-keeping, the way of Christ looked like, as indeed it was, a threat to the whole root and branch of their conception of the good life. And that is why in desperation and fear they felt they must be rid of him.

It is odd, indeed it is tragic, that the good-living and the religious should find themselves in inevitable opposition to the Son of God; but so it was. From their point of view he was dangerous, revolutionary, a threat to their laboriously built structure of goodness. He must go; if need be, he must die. The very men who thought they were serving God and who might be expected to have recognized the Son of God in person became his most implacable enemies.

And this strange bitter opposition between the Spirit of Christ and the spirit of religious righteousness has persisted through the centuries and is with us still today.

We have taken glimpses of what happened when Light and Life and Love visited this earth in person. But the reactions to him, though they are recorded in the Gospel story, could be reproduced any day of the week in any place we care to think of. For neither Christ nor the essential nature of man has changed. His light still shines in the darkness, his voice still calls in the silence, and his way still lies open for those who will dare to follow him.